1

Contents

INTRODUCTION

Whether you live in the city or the country, you've been dreaming about homesteading. Your plans might be pie-in-the-sky dreams or you may be ready to start right this minute, but wherever you are right now, you should know that you can take a step toward your homesteading dreams today.

How do you start a homestead? You don't need to move to a farm to get started with homesteading. Anything you can do to develop more self-sufficiency, cut costs, and live closer to nature will begin moving you in the right direction. Start growing your own food, learn to sew and preserve food, and pick up other valuable skills.

With just a quarter acre of land, you can feed a family of four with fresh, organic food year-round. This comprehensive guide to self-sufficiency gives you all the information you need to grow and preserve a variety of vegetables, fruits, herbs, nuts and grains; raise chickens for eggs and meat; raise cows, sheep and goats for meat or milk; raise pigs and rabbits; and keep honeybees.

Simple instructions make it easy to enjoy canned, frozen, dried and pickled produce all winter; use your own grains to make bread, pasta and beer; turn fresh milk into delicious homemade yogurt, butter and cheese; make your own wine, cordials and herbal teas; and much, much more. It truly is possible to eat entirely from your backyard.

HOMESTEAD OR HOMESTEADING

There are many definitions and ideas of what a homestead is. In a historical context, a "homestead" was defined as a parcel of land (typically 160 acres) that was granted to any US citizen willing to move West to settle on and farm the land for at least five years, as part of the Homestead Act of 1862.

In more modern terms, the act of homesteading is used to describe an agrarian and largely self-sufficient lifestyle. Homesteading activities typically include growing and preserving food crops, cooking meals from scratch, raising animals, making homemade medicines, personal care products, perhaps even clothing, and an overall goal to "live off the land". Homesteaders may also barter and trade for the things they cannot produce themselves.

Homesteaders come in many forms and styles these days. Some homesteaders have acres of land to play with (and maintain), while urban homesteaders are challenged and creative in smaller spaces. There are some hard-core, very traditional homesteaders that attempt to live a fully self-sufficient, zero-waste, off-grid, or near "prepper" status life. Then there are your hobby homesteaders, who are simply drawn to this lifestyle and enjoy it as a light-hearted escape from their usual 9-5 "real life". All versions of homesteading are awesome and acceptable! I'd say we are somewhere in between.

A homestead can mean different things to different people. But in a broad sense, homesteading is about living a self-sufficient lifestyle. For most people, the main aspects of a homestead are owning their land and the buildings on it, and doing small-scale farming with the goal of being self-sufficient, or at least limiting their reliance on outside sources.

Although homesteading typically applies to farms, it's also possible to be an urban homesteader by practicing sustainable living techniques, urban agriculture, and a frugal lifestyle.

Some people believe that homesteading is more defined by the lifestyle choices that you make, rather than whether you live in the country or the city. In the UK, what's called homesteading is often referred to as smallholding. Or less frequently as crofting.

Homesteaders practice subsistence agriculture and often preserve their own food that they harvest to last them through the winter.So skills like canning and pickling are essential for homesteaders to have.

They may even produce their own clothing, textiles, and other crafts. Either to use within their own home or to sell to generate a little bit of extra income.

Homesteading is differentiated from living in a commune or village because of its isolation, both geographically and socially. A homestead typically only houses a single family, or at most, their extended family.Whereas a commune usually has a group of people living together who share responsibilities and possessions but are only loosely connected.

Homesteaders tend to live a more independent life, and may only venture into town once a week or less for supplies or to see friends. This is particularly true for homesteaders who choose not to have a job and get all the income needed to pay for taxes and other expenses from work done on their own land.

Homesteads are far more likely to rely on renewable energy sources like wind or solar electricity than the average home. In addition to growing their own vegetables and livestock, the idea of being completely "off-grid" is a massive appeal to a lot of homesteaders.

STEPS TO START A HOMESTEAD

EVALUATE YOUR PROPERTY

Every property will come with its unique strengths and challenges. When you first set out to start a homestead – what type of property are you working with? Do you already own land, or are you still on the hunt to find a slice of Earth to call your own? Are you currently in your forever home, or do you hope to move again someday soon?

TEMPORARY VS FOREVER

While you will not want to invest a huge amount of money or energy into a rental or temporary space, don't let it stop you from practicing at least some homesteading activities. For example, when we lived in rental accommodations, we still built a couple of raised garden beds. We also grew food in containers, and started composting. This small introduction enabled us to learn some basics of gardening before buying our first home. Just be sure to check with your landlord before doing anything too permanent.

We know this current property isn't our forever home, but we certainly haven't let that stop us from enjoying it to the fullest while we are here! Before we were able to have an extensive garden, we stocked up on seasonal produce at local farmers markets to practice various food preservation techniques. You can also learn to sew, craft, brew kombucha, or make homemade sourdough no matter your living situation.

A four part image collage showing what one can do in a rental property with limited space. The images vary from getting the necessary supplies to build raised beds such as wood and soil, filling the raised bed with soil once it is built, planting out the raised beds with various plants of choice, in this case it was tomatoes, squash, peppers,and basil, and finally using containers to grow vegetables. They can easily be moved and don't take up as much space.

SIZE, RESTRICTIONS, & LAYOUT

Now, think about the property size.A modestly-sized property will be more manageable in regards to maintenance, but may also limit the activities you can do on it such as what types of animals you can raise. Goats, cows, or pigs would not be happy in our 1/5 acre town lot. Nor could we legally keep them. Be sure to familiarize yourself with your town regulations regarding livestock, poultry, bee-keeping, or even things like having a farm stand or collecting rainwater if those are things you're interested in doing.

Now, assuming you do have some property to work with. It's time to make the most of it! Before diving into any permanent projects, be sure to take time to sit back and observe first. For example, you should evaluate an area's sun exposure and source of shade before installing a veggie garden. Also keep in mind how the sun's path will change with the seasons.

Spend time wandering about in your space. How do you want it to eventually look, feel, and function? While nothing needs to be set in stone now, try to dream up your optimal layout – which should be convenient and functional.

A great example of a thoughtful and purposeful layout is through permaculture design, as shown below. You won't want your farm animals directly next to the house. They may be stinky or noisy. Yet you don't want them so far away that it becomes a trek to go visit and care for them, especially if you live in an area with cold winters. Something you will visit frequently, such as a kitchen herb garden, would be ideal just outside the front or back door. Keep your compost area fairly accessible, but not outside your bedroom or kitchen window. I think you get the idea.

MAKE A LIST OF PROJECTS & IDEAS

If you're dreaming to start a homestead, two types of thoughts are likely going through your head. One, you're fantasizing about all of the wonderful, healthy, uber-rewarding things that this new lifestyle will bring you. And it will! I promise. But two You are also fretting over all the skills, tools, money, time, or other resources you may not have to make all of those dreams come true right now. Here is the deal: pretty much no one does. Not right at first, and not all at once.

Remember that creating a homestead is a process, and this is just the start.

Example Homesteading Projects & Goals

• Create a veggie garden space

• Plant an herb garden

• Plant fruit trees or an orchard

• Start a compost area, worm bin, compost tumbler (or all of the above)

• Create a pollinator bed, area, or even a meadow full of flowers

• Learn how to ferment, can, dehydrate and/or pickle your harvests

• Adopt chickens, goats, sheep, rabbits, pigs, cows, or other "farm animals"

• Build a barn, stables, or other auxiliary structures

• Create a root cellar or large pantry

• Learn how to make kombucha, homemade sourdough, apple cider vinegar, homemade seasonings, vegetable (or bone) broth, and other useful staples

• Learn how to make natural medicine like Fire Cider and Elderberry Syrup, or personal care products like calendula oil, soap, lotions.

- Start a beehive

- Learn how to sew, knit, crochet, or use natural dyes

- Turn your property in to a Certified Wildlife Habitat

- Build or install a greenhouse or hoop house

- Set up a rainwater collection system system

- Learn how to make compost tea

- Start a farm stand

- Sell homemade goods locally or online

- Host workshops, classes, or homestays to share your knowledge and skills with others

A hand is holding a National Wildlife Federation Certified Wildlife Habitat plaque in front of a view of the front yard garden. There isn't a lot of open space with many plants for pollinators, raised beds for vegetables, shrubs, and trees spaced throughout the area.

A wonderful long-term goal is to turn your property into an ecosystem of its own. But there are usually many smaller (manageable) projects and steps along the way to get there.

PRIORITIZE

Now take just one or two manageable projects at a time, and forget everything else on the list for a while. It is 100% unrealistic (and 7000% stressful) to try and do everything at once, within a year, or even within a couple of years! That is, unless you are diving in to start a homestead full-time with unlimited resources and help. Where to begin? Well, your priorities are personal. This journey to start a homestead is all about what you want to do, and when you want to do it. There are no rules.

Will this simply be a hobby homestead, or do you intend to make a living from your land? That will obviously influence how seriously or quickly you approach projects, and which ones to focus on first.For example, do you hope to sell eggs locally? Then building a secure chicken coop and establishing a flock will be at the top of your list.

Certain homestead projects will dictate the order or timeline for others. For instance, you shouldn't set up a beehive until you have a healthy pollinator garden, orchard, or other nectar and pollen-producing plants established first. Circumstance will also drive your priorities. Like: "Oh crap, the irrigation line broke! I guess it is time to brush up on our plumbing skills..." Or that moment when your kitchen counter is overflowing with homegrown tomatoes, but you've never preserved tomatoes before. Evidently, the time to dive in and learn is now.

IDEAS FOR THE SUB URBAN (OR URBAN) HOMESTEAD

Put in a Garden

Regardless of whether your yard space is big or small, it is almost always possible to find at least a little spot where you can plant some veggies. Choose heirloom varieties that aren't available in your local stores (this year we grew Yukon Gold potatoes, since we usually only have access to Russets. It was a delicious change of pace!). Find out what varieties of vegetables thrive in shade and sun. With a little creativity, you should be able to maximize the harvest from any sized garden plot. And of course, like the apartment homesteader, you can always use containers and pots to grow a variety of edibles.

Compost

If you've read the story of my journey into homesteading and natural living, then you know that it all began with a compost pile! Turn your coffee grounds, egg shells, and kitchen scraps into valuable (and frugal) food for your urban farm garden. The sky is the limit when it comes to composting set-ups. Build your own bins, use re-purposed materials (trash cans, plastic storage totes, etc) or purchase ready-made composting buckets or tumblers. Use your rich compost to amend your garden plot, raised beds, or containers.

Become a Bee Keeper

While this may seem like a stretch for some folks, more and more people are becoming backyard beekeepers. My cousin keeps a thriving hive in her very suburban backyard, which provides her family with delicious local, raw honey. And if you have children or grandchildren, just think of all the science experiments and hands-on learning that a backyard hive could provide.

Landscape with Edibles

Water is a precious commodity in the part of Wyoming where we live. Even though we have our own well and no water restrictions, I just can't bring myself to pour water on a lawn (or even flowers...) that only live a few months and give us nothing to eat in return. It feels like such a waste. So, when I have an empty flower bed, I resist the urge to buy expensive annuals, and instead try to plant edibles in their place. This year, my "flower" beds around the house held sunflowers, tomatoes, basil, lettuce, and spinach. It's still green, it's still beautiful (to me anyway), and I feel better when I water it, knowing that it will help contribute to my family's food needs. I'm not necessarily recommending that you rip out your entire yard overnight, but next time you head to the garden store, consider choosing fruit trees/bushes, herbs, or vegetables instead of annual flowers that will be dead in a short time.

Consider Chickens

More and more cities and towns across the U.S. are allowing their residents take part in urban agriculture by keeping backyard chickens. If it is allowed by your homeowner's association, I highly recommend considering a small flock of your own. From eggs and meat, to extra fertilizer and sheer entertainment, there are many reasons to become a chicken farmer in your own backyard.

Transform your Kitchen into a Homesteader's Kitchen

No matter what type of homesteading you do, food production and preservation is a HUGE part of it. Get busy learning how to make your own breads and cheeses. Learn how to can and preserve the fresh produce you find at your farmer's market. If you have room in your basement or garage, consider purchasing an upright or chest freezer to hold frozen fruits/veggies, make-aheads like pie fillings, homemade broth, and beans, frozen eggs from your backyard chickens, and grassfed poultry, beef, pork, or wild game (buying in bulk is usually a more frugal option).

Keep Worms

Compost worms are a wonderful way to put your kitchen scraps to good use, AND gain some new creepy crawly friends. Here's a helpful post that highlights everything you need to know about feeding your new wormy buddies.

To me, there is one defining characteristic of all successful homesteaders, whether they be apartment dwellers, urban, suburban, semi-rural, or rural:

A successful homesteader know how to make do with what they have and think outside of the box.

WHERE TO START

Pick one or two projects that you can start in the next month or so. For example, if you live in the suburbs, you might want to get a few laying hens to keep for eggs. You'll need to research how to raise chickens, find out your local laws to make sure it's legal, plan for a chicken coop and then buy or build one, and order baby chicks or buy older pullets or hens. That's enough to keep you plenty busy for an entire season.

If that seems like too much, start smaller. Have a fireplace?Consider putting in an insert for wood heat. Have a sunny windowsill? Grow some lettuce and herbs for salads and cooking.Have a nice-sized backyard? Put in raised beds and plant a veggie garden this season.

Research

Besides starting a small project or two this season, take the time to read up about homesteading skills. You can go with a compendium-style book like The

Encyclopedia of Country Living, or something more focused like Root Cellaring. The Weekend Homesteader is a great place to begin, as it breaks down projects into tasks that can be completed in a weekend, and you'll find projects that are a fit even if you're a suburbanite. Take a look at more great homesteading books and consider subscribing to one of these small farm magazines.

Define Priorities

Once you've soaked up as much information as possible about how to homestead, you'll be itching to start planning your homestead, but you've got to get your priorities in order. There are many facets to homesteading: growing and preserving your own food, raising animals (or not), and producing your own energy are among the bigger goals that most aspiring homesteaders have.

You'll want to consider which of these is most important to you so you can focus your energies appropriately. For example, if energy sufficiency is at the top of your list, you might choose to convert a diesel car and begin running it on waste vegetable oil or outfit your suburban home with solar panels before even buying land. If you know your heart is with raising animals for meat and egg production, and you're okay living on-grid for a few years while you do that, this information is going to dictate your next steps.

Identify a Property

For many of us, finding that "place in the country" is a key part of homesteading. Buying land may have made it to the top of your list of priorities. If so, start looking. It can take time to find a good piece of land suitable for homesteading. Remember that you don't need 40 acres, or even 10, to have a homestead. Even a small acreage such as 2 or 4 acres can provide for a family. However, if you want to use the land as a woodlot (see energy sufficiency above), 20 to 40 acres may be more appropriate.

Plan the First Year

Planning your first year on your homestead, whether you're doing that in place, in the suburbs, or city. If you can look ahead to a move, whether it's a work in progress or still in fantasy land, that can help you move from dream to reality.

STEPS TO START HOMESTEADING ON THE CHEAP

Simplify your life

This would be the first thing to do when you want to start homesteading. Sometimes we get caught up thinking we always need to be doing more, when in fact doing less but doing it really well, is a much better (and cheaper) way to go. Is there anything in your life that is draining your time, energy, and money that you could eliminate or cut back? Maybe your kids are signed up for a few too many activities. Maybe you are a member of a book club, have a side hustle, go to the gym every day, and volunteer at the library. Those are all good things, but you can't always add more and add more, sometimes you need to cut a few things. So if you are really serious about homesteading, realize that it is a time commitment. You will end up frustrated and disappointed if you try to ADD homesteading without taking anything else out.

Make homesteading friends

Homesteading is significantly easier if you have some buddies for a lot of reasons. One is that it's nice to have some support when you need it. If all you ever hear from people is how crazy you are for homesteading, and you don't have anyone to talk to that agrees with your craziness, you're going to get burnt out.

Another reason is that it's nice to partner up sometimes. Let's say you are really good at growing tomatoes, and you have a neighbor with too many laying chickens. This is a no brainer right? Trading is something that homesteaders love.

Number three would be that you are going to have homesteading questions. The best people to ask those questions are experienced homesteaders in your area. Weather, climate, laws, etc are things best answered by someone who lives right where you do.

And fourth, to save the most money possible, you must borrow things. It's nothing to be ashamed of, it's just a smart thing to do. If you don't have the money to buy something, ask a friend if you can borrow theirs when they aren't using it. Every year I borrow a canner from my mother in law, a juicer from my aunt, and a dehydrator from my friend. I also had another friend give me her old canning supplies because she didn't need them after all her kids were moved out. Make friends! Just do it.

Start gardening

This is the first homesteading thing I did in my adult life. That might have something to do with the fact that I studied permaculture as a teenager, but still. Dirt is one of my favorite things in the world, that might have something to do with it too.

You can start gardening for about $5 really. All you need is some dirt, sun, water, and a packet of seeds. It DOES NOT have to be special dirt. Contrary to what some people believe, seeds do grow in almost any old soil. You might not have the same size tomato plants as your neighbor who uses miracle grow, but your seeds will still grow. A shovel is handy, but if you don't already have one you can borrow a friends, or grow a "no-till" garden. If you have literally no piece of dirt/land to grow some seeds in, get creative. Use pots, sign up for a spot in the community garden, or better yet, BORROW a few feet in your friends yard. Seriously, I can't think of a single homesteader that wouldn't let you share a tiny piece of their garden if you are willing to take care of it.

Preserve what you grow and what you gather

Preserving food is a dying art. There are a million ways to preserve fruits, veggies, meat, nuts, and everything else. The whole point of it is to save the food you have from going bad and wasting.What better way is there to save money than figuring out ways to use everything that you already have?

The 4 biggest ways that I preserve food are canning, freezing, dehydrating, and cold storage. You can borrow canning supplies, but you will need to purchase canning jars unless you know someone who has extra. You can borrow a dehydrator, though I feel like dehydrators pay for themselves in the first one or two uses honestly. If you don't have a freezer then you may want to wait on that one since they are hard to find for less than a few hundred dollars. As for cold storage, if you don't have space in a basement or under your house, you can literally dig a hole in the ground.

Don't think that you can't preserve food if you don't grow a large garden. More than half the food that I preserve comes from somewhere other than my own yard. Check out this post on How to get free produce to learn how I get food to fill my freezer and my canning jars every year for free.

Learn to sew

Sewing is not an all or nothing activity. You do not have to sew all of your kids clothes to save money. Every little bit counts. If you don't own a sewing machine, that's okay. Although it is easier and faster with a sewing machine, you can start out with small things that only require a needle and thread.Take for example mending your husbands pants instead of buying new ones. How about letting out the hem to your growing sons pants so they fit for a few more months.

To me, sewing and mending is one of the best examples of "making it work". It is an incredibly valuable homesteading skill that saves you money. Make it a goal to learn at least basic sewing skills.

Get starts from other people

Growing things is a big part of homesteading, whether that is plants, animals, or a family. Plants and animals cost money. But almost everything that grows, is multiplying and growing more. Plants send up shoots, drop seeds, or re-root themselves.Animals have babies. Instead of buying everything you need to grow plants or raise animals, get your "starts" from your friends and neighbors.Ask your friends what things they have extra of, or what things are always producing more then they need. Here are a few examples of things that are all over the place where I live:

Plan ahead

I am a procrastinator to the extreme. I know I am, and I try to fix it, but the fact is that I will probably struggle with it forever. When it comes to homesteading, procrastinating costs you money, time, and problems. Make lists, have a calendar, plan meals, draw out your garden. The more you plan, the better you can manage your time, and the more money you will save.

Let's look at an extreme example: think about what a difference it would make if you were to plan out an entire year of meals. I have never heard of anyone doing this, but humor me for a minute. You could plan out your garden for exactly what food you would need to grow. You would know how much of each thing you needed to preserve. And you could save a ton of time always having things ready for your meals. Now I know that was an extreme example, but if you fall anywhere in the middle, you are still on your way to some pretty great homesteading, planning ahead, and saving money. And that goes for anything, not just food. Plan ahead what tools and supplies you will need for the whole year. You could be asking friends early on, or keeping your eyes out for those things at the thrift store.Think about it.

Cheap chickens

I call them that because they are. Farmer and I started our chicken adventure with $26. We built a little house out of scrap wood, and we kept them in a box in the laundry room before they were big enough to live outside. The baby chicks cost us $16 for 8, and a bag of starter feed cost $10. We let them free range after that. Cheap, cheap, cheap.And they are an easy animal to start out with if you don't have any experience.

Compost

Starting a compost pile doesn't cost a dime.Just start throwing everything compostable into a pile, and water and churn it every once in awhile.Composting is not a complicated thing and it's really hard to get it wrong.But the benefits of having your own compost is a more productive and healthy garden, and free fertilizer. Add some of the chicken poop from your new chickens to your pile and you will really have some black gold.

Quit buying things you can't afford

Part of homesteading is being frugal. The easiest way to blow through money is to buy things you can't afford. I say that because when you put things on payments, you end up spending way more money on something just because you couldn't wait a few months. Make a rule for yourself that you won't buy anything unless you have the cash for it. Sometimes that means waiting awhile yes.But there are more benefits to that habit than just saving money. Peace of mind, better relationships with your family, and more trust from the people you have money dealings with are some of the ones Farmer and I have noticed.

HOW A FARM DIFFER FROM A HOMESTEAD

A farm generates money by selling the livestock and/or produce from the land. Like the definition, it is about production.a farmer has a different goal than a homesteader in that he/she strives to make a living or at least bring in some income. One can be a conventional farmer or a more sustainable farmer. Most people will equate a farmer to soybeans and corn, but there is obviously much more to it than that. One of our goals here is to generate enough income to make a living off of the farm. But, we also have another goal.Read on.

A homestead is a place where a person and/or family cultivates the land and tries to become more self sufficient. A homesteader strives to live off of the land by growing and raising what he eats. Although they might sell a few things here or there, that really isn't there primary goal. They are the 'back-to-the-land' kind of people who appreciate the organic or close to it growing measures. They like to use what they can on their land to make it more sustainable.

Sometimes farmers can lose sight of a more sustainable approach and just get caught up in the more conventional ways to farm. Their creativity can diminish and their only goal is to make enough money.

Sometimes, homesteaders can get so caught up in living off of the land, that they forget that there are numerous ways to make a little cash to help keep things rolling.

With many things in life, I kind of like the balanced approach. Our goal here at the farm is to not only generate income, but to live off the land by consuming what we grow and use what we have without relying on outside resources as much as possible.

I think there should be a different word for this type of person like myself. Because of the many misconceptions of farmers today, another word needs to be added to distinguish us from the rest.

HOMESTEADER STRUCTURES

And if you really want to get the most out of your scarce resources, you have to build structures to get the job done. Here are four great structures every homesteader should build.

Root Cellar

If you're a successful gardener, one of the challenges you'll have is storing everything after the harvest. As fun as canning is, you don't want to can everything, right? One of the best and simplest ways to store produce is with a root cellar. A root cellar is a structure built into the ground or an existing basement.

It takes advantage of the ground's naturally cool temperature and high humidity, and allows you to store fresh vegetables for months at a time. Vegetables can be placed in the root storage with minimal preparation, so it can save you time for other tasks. Root crops such as potatoes, beets and onions are great candidates for a root cellar; fruits like apples will stay fresh for a long time in root cellar storage, too.

BarnIf you're a homesteader, you need a barn of some sort. Even if it's a small one, a barn serves many critical purposes. If you don't have an outbuilding, getting work done consistently can be challenging. You need a dry place to store your hay and animal feeds. You need somewhere out of the weather to manage key livestock tasks, like milking goats or cows. Barns also make it easier to organize your important tools and keep them handy. And a barn is a great place to retreat to with a cup of coffee – or to just take a break.

Cold frames

You don't have to let the seasons curtail your gardening. Cold frames can help you start gardening in the spring, and extend your harvest well past the first frost. A cold frame is typically a sealed wooden or brick box with a glass lid that opens. They can help insulate plants and keep them warmer when temperatures outside are less than plant friendly. Some people even heat their cold frames by adding a base of rotting compost, which gives off heat. If you're in a hurry, you can buy your cold frames online. However, they also are a fun and easy building project, too.

Compost pile

A good homesteader never lets anything go to waste. And if you have a compost pile, you can literally turn your trash into a treasure. A compost pile lets you save nearly anything – from kitchen scraps, to paper, to grass clippings – and turn them into something that can improve your garden soil substantially. Recycling your trash into compost also can save you money, too; if everything is ending up in the compost pile, it will help you spend less on things like garbage bags and trash pickup. There are many types of composting systems out there. Figure out which one is good for you, and give composting a try.

Final Thoughts

Successful homesteaders make everything count. And these four structures can help you get the most out of your homestead. Depending on your thriftiness and building skills, you can make all these structures with re-purposed materials for a relatively low price. However, if you're in a hurry, you can buy them all as kits, too. Regardless of how you get there, each one of these structures can make you a more productive homesteader. So, start planning now, and get these structures built as soon as you can.

THINGS TO CONSIDER TO GET THE PERFECT LAND FOR HOMESTEADING

Some things to consider in your search for the perfect piece of land include:

Property Rights

Would you own the mineral rights and water rights for the property? Don't assume when you're making an offer. Check the deed for any restrictions, rights of way, or easements that could prevent you from fully using your land.

Acreage

It might seem like you want as much land as you can afford. But more isn't necessarily always better. You don't want more land than you can maintain. Wooded land is ideal since it doesn't need to be maintained like a pasture does, and you can either use the firewood for heat or sell it for some extra income.

Water

Ideally, you want at least one natural water source like a pond or creek that doesn't run dry seasonally. That way you'll always have access to water.

You also want to know the age and condition of any existing underground well on the property, as drilling a new one can be costly.

COMMON HOMESTEADING ACTIVITIES

Here are some common homesteading activities to let you know what to expect day-to-day.

• Sustainable energy generation

• Keeping livestock (chicken, goats, pigs, cows, bees, etc.)

• Preserving and canning

• Fishing and hunting

• Maintaining tractors and other equipment

• Chopping firewood and forestry

• Producing milk products like cheese and butter.

WHY YOU SHOULD START A HOMESTEAD

Start A Homestead

Homesteading has a number of legal and financial benefits, as well as the potential to increase your quality of life and satisfaction.

Homestead Exemptions

In some US states, homesteaders can make use of something called a homestead exemption. This allows homeowners to protect the value of their home and land from creditors and taxes.

This benefit also transfers on to a spouse if the homeowner dies. Homestead benefits are for the life of you and your spouse, as long as you continue to occupy the homestead property. That means homesteading can potentially give you something called forced sale immunity. That means creditors can't force you to sell your home to cover your debts if you default on a loan or other debt. However, this usually won't protect you from specific types of debt like defaulted property taxes or a mortgage foreclosure.

Some states allow your entire property to be exempt from property taxes. In other cases, you're shielded up to a specific amount, such as the first $50,000 or $75,000 of your home's assessed value.

Since homestead exemptions vary so much from state to state, you should consult a lawyer or accountant before making any financial decisions related to your homestead.

Security

Having the title to your land and home gives many homesteaders a greater sense of security. With minimal costs and expenses, and the ability to be self-sufficient and live off the land, homesteading can provide you with a feeling of safety. By living the homesteading lifestyle, you'll naturally have lower bills.

Homesteaders tend to make lower income, but since they have much lower expenses they may not even need to work a conventional job.

Pride

Homesteaders take pride in having a piece of land to call their own. Most couldn't imagine renting a tiny apartment, and prefer to have their own land where they can provide for their family.

Less Stress

Like most people who live in the country, homesteaders report experiencing a lot less stress than those who live in loud and busy cities and urban centers. Imagine your home being surrounded by the sounds of birds chirping and livestock, instead of busy traffic and police sirens.

More Environmentally Conscious

Homesteaders have a closer relationship to nature than those who live in the city.They know where their food comes from, because they often grow most of it themselves. As a result, they naturally have an incentive to care more about the environment and make sure their agriculture practices are sustainable.

That way their land will continue to support them for the rest of their lives, and hopefully the lives of their children as well.

Better Physical Health

Running a homestead requires a lot more physical labor than an office job, or most jobs in the city for that matter. Combine that with the fact that homesteaders typically eat healthy nutritious foods they make themselves, and have much less opportunity to indulge in processed foods like pizza or chips.

Lower stress, regular physical exercise, and a healthy diet are all strong factors in staying fit well into old age, and living a long life.

Increased Self-Confidence

Starting a homestead will require picking up a whole set of new skills and hobbies that you never had before. These new skills will make you more capable and self-sufficient. And as a result, your confidence in yourself and self-esteem will probably rise dramatically.

Homesteading isn't easy. In fact, there's a steep learning curve to learn all of the new skills you'll need. It can be challenging and even overwhelming at first. But many of these challenges will help to grow you into a stronger person. It's a very empowering feeling to know that you're self-sufficient and completely in control of your own destiny.

For many homesteaders, society and the electric grid could disappear tomorrow, and they'd still be able to continue on enjoying exactly the same lifestyle.

Family Bonding

Homesteading can bring your family closer together. Imagine not having to go work at a job all day any more. Instead, you can spend your day doing chores and taking care of your property alongside your spouse and kids. That means a lot more opportunities for chatting and getting quality time for each other.

Homesteading won't magically create the perfect family. You're still likely to have disagreements and time when you want your own space. But a family that spends time together during the day and sits down to enjoy a meal together when it's all said and done is likely to be closer to one another because of it.

REASONS TO START HOMESTEADING TODAY

It connects you with your food

Our society is disturbingly unaware of how our food arrives on our table. Kids don't have a clue their hamburger once had eyes and a nose, or that their french fries grew in the ground (in dirt...).

Homesteading breaks this cycle by getting our fingernails dirty and encouraging us to return to an intimate relationship with the cycles of nature and food production. I'm convinced this is a need every human carries, and returning to it satisfies something deep inside us.

It tastes good

So I lied a little up there in point #1. The whole reconnecting with nature thing is only part of the reason we raise our own food. The other reason is because it just plain tastes good.

Juicy red strawberries picked mere seconds before landing on your tastebuds, happy brown eggs with full-flavored yellow yolks, frothy fresh milk with a five-inch creamline to be turned into golden butter.

Homesteading brings freedom

We homesteaders tend to be an independent bunch, and our self-sufficient tendencies are usually the primary factors leading us down this unconventional path. Homesteading can provide freedom from a centralized food supply and even freedom from the power grid, if you choose that route.

When people start complaining about the rising prices of dairy products? I simply grin and give our milk cow an extra flake of hay and a pat on the head. When the news starts chattering about how beef prices will skyrocket?I feel secure knowing we have two steers out in the pasture, and one in the freezer.

And this increased measure of freedom from the price-hikes at the grocery store makes this wildly-independent homesteader girl's heart happy. It's a good reason to start homesteading today.

It provides security during hard times

Whether your concern is a small emergency (such as a job loss), or a big one (you know, the whole zombie thing...), homesteading provides a reassuring measure of security in both the areas of food and skills.

Most homesteaders keep an impressive supply of food on hand because: a) When you grow your own food, you almost always have a surplus to preserve. b) Most of us have a strange addiction to mason jars and canning (we can't help it). While our own personal preparedness measures still need a little polishing, we always have enough food to last for many months, tucked away in our pantry, basement, cupboards, and freezer. Plus, it's reassuring to know many of the skills we possess (such as gardening, hunting/butchering, milking, food preservation) would help carry us through in an extreme survival scenario.

It's hard

Yes.I did mean to include this one on the list. Us modern-folk have it so easy... Too easy. I'm convinced humans need an element of struggle and challenge to stay satisfied. We need something to strive for. We need to see achievement. Homesteading is a struggle.It's messy.And sweaty.And hard.And gritty.Yet the satisfaction you gain when you push through the tough stuff is incomparable.

It's one of the best ways to raise kids

My kids think everyone has a milk cow. When you run out of milk, you go down to the barn and get more. Of course. Their eyes light up whenever they shove on their tiny mud boots and wander down to the coop to check for eggs (usually getting sidetracked with various other adventures in the process).

THE GREAT BENEFITS OF HOMESTEADING

Homesteading is humbling

As a homesteader, one quickly realizes just how small one is and how finite life is. For any homesteader, mistakes will be overwhelming. Animals will die. Crops will be ruined. Structures fall down. Plans fall through. It's humbling to attempt and tame a piece of this Earth, only to have it implode time after time. Which hear me now it will. The chickens may be eaten by an owl or the cow may stick her food in the milk bucket — but regardless of the failings that will inevitable come, homesteading continues. So while it may be an extremely humbling road to wander down, the perseverance bred through the humbling failures is not to be missed. It's character building, don't you think? To fail, recognize one's inability to control life, pray for grace, and then continue on.

Homesteading builds a strong work ethic

Work ethic is something strongly missing in our culture, don't you think? I've recently been rereading Farmer Boy and am taken back by the amount of work that was expected of children. At the ripe 'ol age of six?seven? they're milking cows. Feeding animals.Training oxen. Cooking supper alongside their Mom. Kids are CAPABLE and thrive in such environments. While I'm thankful that our lifestyle no longer requires such labor from our children, it's important that the idea of building up ourselves (and our children) with strong work ethics isn't thrown out with the bathwater.

If anything will build up a solid work ethic, it's the responsibility that comes with growing food so that our family can eat or raising animals that are reliant on us, day after day, for their survival.

The instant negativity associated with laziness in instantly felt on the homestead. The best way to breed it out is to slather it in work.

Homesteading tastes good

Many of y'all are chicken owners you know the beautiful, orange, perky yolks that come from a well-loved and healthy hen. The taste is indistinguishable. I've ever surprised (why? I don't know) at the incredibly depth of difference of homegrown food to conventional food. Again, I think it's important to note: I'm very thankful that my survival is not dependent on my own ability to produce food. I think it's important and progressive that we have such food available to us year-round. But that being said, a lot of it just ain't good. Ever tasted an out-of-season-picked-green-raspberry? It's like a flavorless gob of nastiness.

Even my hard to convince husband was undoubtedly convinced at our last dinner date out – he ordered the roast chicken. "Well, it sure isn't like our Rainbow Rangers. It's sort of flat tasting and squishy."(You can read more about meat chickens here.) I felt the same about my steak, which was cooked and flavored beautifully, but still fell incredibly short of the grass-fed local meat we're used to. We spent the rest of the dinner planning how we could grow MORE of these things ourselves if for no other reason than the taste.

Homesteading breeds appreciation

Back to those fresh tomatoes. Remember the first one you ate out of your garden last year? I bet you do. Because before you could taste that first tomato, you had to put in months of work planting seeds, caring for tender seedlings, planning the proper time to plant them out, protecting them from harsh weather, nurturing them as they grew and blossomed, trellising them as they became heavy with fruit, and patiently waiting for them finally ripen. And when that first delicious orb is removed from the vine, it's hard to not be brought to tears. I guarantee you that after hand milking a cow, you'll never look at a gallon of milk the same way, and the same goes for millions of tasks on the homestead.

Nothing breeds appreciation like knowing the hard work that went into providing our family with something. I think this also correlates very closely with the homesteading mantra: "Use it up, wear it out, make it do, or do without". When the items that one grows or produces holds such extreme value, they tend to be treated far better and made to last, as well as utilized to their maximum. It's hard to find homesteaders that are wasteful – they appreciate the value of everything (even if it's garden scraps or manure for the compost pile).

Homesteading adds a new value to meat

If you've ever grown your own your own meat, you know two things: Meat takes an incredible amount of energy (ie: feedstuff) to raise and Taking the life of the animal you are raising for meat is hard.

Let's start with the first point the amount of energy it takes to raise meat. Whether this be in the form of grass or grain, the amount it takes to raise the mean is quite astounding. Because of this, we've found that the amount of meat that we eat has been greatly affected. We don't eat it at every meal.We don't even eat it every day. Limited resources of energy in the form of feed means limited amount of meat. Because vegetables and eggs can be grown here with such fewer resources than meat, that's a huge portion of what we eat. They are easier, cheaper, and require less energy to produce. Not something one really has to think about when purchasing meat from the store, but for a homestead, it's a really important equation to consider.

Taking the life of our meat animals also adds a new value to eating this protein. As was the case with our rabbits and our chickens, it was with great sadness and a profound appreciation that we slaughtered and butchered them for our consumption. It's not something to be taken lightly and when we've actually had to do the raising, killing, and processing of the animals ourselves we've found the meat to be far more valuable to us. You can read more about why we morally agree with eating meat HERE.

Homesteading develops a truer sense of gender roles

We hold to a Biblical view and belief of gender roles and life on the homestead has proven those gender roles to be so true and necessary. Stuart is so strong and capable of many of the manual labor tasks that I am physically incapable of. I wish I was buffer – but I ain't. And so it goes. While nursing Owen, catering to nap schedules, preserving food, and preparing meals, I find myself naturally more drawn to work in the home (or that which can be done in the garden or in the coop with the children). While this isn't always the case (as I often lend Stuart a hand with big projects, bucking hay, or building fence) it's given me a new appreciation for my role as a Christian woman and as a wife, helpmeet, and mother.

I see great value in the chores that not only keep this homesteading running but also are of great service to this family. Life on the homestead has caused me to see how these roles became so defined in times past – I picture a woman with a child on each hip, a giant white apron smeared with kitchen projects, and a few chickens following her around the yard. It's a beautiful thing and in no way less meaningful or important. All work on the homestead is extremely valuable and all of it is required to keep it running smoothly.

Homesteading increases knowledge

Like anything you commit time and energy to, naturally, knowledge is gained on the subject matter. Running a homestead has been no different. We've learned about everything from native grasses, to feed conversions, to heritage breeds, to the patterns and cycles of the honey bee, to milking a dairy cow, to fencing options, to soil assessments, to composting, to pollination, to cheese making, to water and energy usage, to first aid, to gutting a chicken, and everything in between.

One year ago, I had no idea how to do almost all of the homesteading tasks that I am capable of today. Knowledge is gained from other homesteaders, the internet, a variety of books and hands on work. It's a steep learning process full of common sense and practical knowledge.

Homesteading breeds dreams

As of yet, we've never found that nirvana of perfection with our homestead. We're always looking forward to what we can do better, more efficiently, and with improved results. Once we are successful with one project, it's time to expand the operation and dream bigger. I love to dream.It's one of my favorite past times. It keeps us working and hopeful for what is to come!

While these great benefits of homesteading may not be true for every homesteader, we've found them to be very true to ours. At the risk of sounding cliche, homesteading has developed our character and grown us into better people of faith. We rely on the Lord for all the happenings every day on the homestead and are so thankful for every day that we get to continue on this journey with our land and our animals.

BACKYARD HOMESTEADING

The backyard homesteading movement is about sustainability, self sufficiency, vintage skills and reclaiming a vibrant part of our history well that is what it means to me. Your reasons might be very different. Whatever your reasons I encourage you to start – the hardest step you'll take is the first one.

Backyard Homesteading addresses the needs of many people who want to take control of the food they eat and the products they use--even if they live in a urban or suburban house on a typical-size lot. It shows homeowners how to turn their yard into a productive and wholesome "homestead" that allows them to grow their own fruits and vegetables, and raise farm animals.

STEPS INTO BACKYARD HOMESTEADING

Some call it backyard homesteading but you may have heard other names like, urban homesteading, suburban homesteading or backyard farming. But the basics of backyard homesteading are the same – taking the space you have and raising food on it and reclaiming vintage skills.

It's funny that in 2014 it has become a somewhat trendy thing to do; as if it's a revolutionary idea. But, in truth, this is really taking a concept that has been part of our lives until the last few decades and making it work in today's home. From the meat rabbits of the great depression to the victory gardens of the World Wars; backyard homesteading has been a tried and true way of life.

Start a garden

This can feel challenging if you've never gardened before. Don't fear, it is really as easy as finding out what grows in your area and when, then start planning. Check with your local extension office for a planting calendar. My main gardening style is Square Foot Gardening – less space and more veggies! I started with 1 4×4 garden box and now I have 8 – add as you're feeling comfortable and confident.

If you're in an apartment consider container gardening. I use containers, like self-watering buckets and fabric pots, to extend my growing space onto my porch. I have had wonderful success using these buckets for peppers, tomatoes and even kale. But I don't use them in the summer because the summer heat in Phoenix makes the root base too hot. Remember to buy good, non-gmo, organic seeds! And good soil – a strong, healthy base is essential.

Start Composting

Composting has so many benefits less trash, healthier soil, etc. And it really isn't the daunting task you might think it is. You can even build your own trash can composter (seriously if I can, you can). Then start adding kitchen scraps, bunny droppings, coffee grounds and even egg shells. Mix in a bit of leaves, grass clippings and you're off to the races! It isn't rocket science...more like biology.

I'm sure your first thought will be chickens, and they are great. Chickens provide much more than eggs. Their waste can be composted, they'll work your compost if you let them and they are natural pest control. Unfortunately we all don't have the space for them in our backyards and not all cities allow them.

Another awesome option is quail. The Coturnix quail only needs 1 square foot of space, though more is appreciated. Hens will start laying around 8 weeks of age and generally lay an egg a day. You'll need about 3-4 of their eggs to equal one chicken egg but boy are they worth it; creamy and delicious!

Quail hens are virtual noise free – unlike chickens who sing their egg song loud & proud. Now the roos are a bit nosier, and I was so over ours after about a week. But you don't need a rooster for yummy eggs. You can keep your quail inside in cages but they do great on the ground as cage-free birds too.

Raise some Backyard Meat

The best meat you'll ever eat is the one you raise. Why? You, as the producer, decide the environment, quality of life and feed that animal receives. Now, chances are, you're not going to be raising a cow or a pig in your backyard...but there are other options.

Chickens – not a bad choice but if you can keep chickens then you'll probably want layers versus meat birds. The space and time required for meat chickens can make them problematic in an ordinary backyard. Because of this I'm not going to go into much on chickens for this article.

Quails – an excellent choice for poultry meat. Hatch to butcher is about 8 weeks and won't require much space. Quail are also much easier to process as well; a sharp pair of scissors are all you really need. Most people don't pluck their quail either just simply skin them and they are ready to go. If you're serious about raising quail for a meat source you'll want to consider getting an incubator instead of buying chicks from someone else. The incubator will quickly pay for itself and may make the rooster worth his noise (you may want to get your neighbor some eggs/meat).

Rabbits – the other white meat. Seriously though, rabbits are an excellent meat source for the backyard (apartment) homesteader. They reproduce rapidly and provide an excellent lean white meat at about 8 – 12 weeks, depending on the breed. A single doe can produce a 1,000 times her weight in meat every year; you'll never see those kind of results from any other livestock! A breeding trio could easily keep a family of 4 stocked up on rabbit meat for entire year. Processing takes about 15 minutes start to finish and the cull is quick. Keeping rabbits will be great for your garden too – rabbit droppings are easy compost additions!

CONCLUSION

It can be hard to figure out where to start. You may wonder what to do first, especially if you know nothing about owning land, farming, or going off-grid for energy. This article seeks to demystify this a bit and give you some concrete first steps to take that will begin your homesteading journey right now.

Homesteading is a big commitment, but absolutely worth it in my opinion. It's empowering to become more self-sufficient. It's stress-relieving, (scientifically proven) to grow a garden. Homesteading also saves a lot of money, if you do it the right way.

If you're a homesteader, optimizing is important. You must stretch the growing season out as far as you can. You need to maximize the space to store your tools, hay and livestock feed. You must make the crops you just harvested last through the winter. And you don't want to waste anything, even your trash.

Homesteading has transformed me as a person in so many ways. I'll never look at soil, or milk, or eggs, or meat the same way again. So many aspects of life are more clear as I've become more aware of the cycles of nature.

My palate has improved as I've learned how to grow, prepare, and enjoy food with deep flavors. My confidence has grown as I've done things which previously seemed unattainable. I am completely convinced pursuing a modern homesteading lifestyle, and becoming more intentional in how we live and eat, is one of the most satisfying and empowering things a person can do.

41437281R00046